Joyful Poems for children
Psalm 100:1-3

Wanda & Kadeedra Young

Please email: Wanda D. Young at
youngman1134@aol.com
for more copies of this book and
Inspired Spiritual Poems written by Wanda D. Young.

©2007 Wanda D. Young Publishers

ISBN: 978-1-933594-66-8

All rights reserved. No part of this book may be reproduced in any format without express permission from the authors.

Printed in the USA by
Faith Baptist Church Publications
Fort Pierce, FL 34982
www.fbcpublications.com

Dedication

This book is dedicated to our
daughter Kadeedra Young.
Her sweet relationship with her Lord,
and her willingness to allow the Lord to
work in her life is shown in the poetry
written by Her in this book.
It has been our privilege
to see our daughter grow and
rejoice with her mother in the Lord.
We give thanks to our Lord
and Saviour Jesus Christ for the unspeakable
Gift of this wonderful little girl.

Her loving parents,
Pastor Sterling and Wanda Young

Make a joyful noise unto the LORD, all ye lands. Serve the LORD with gladness: come before his presence with singing. Know ye that the LORD he is God: it is he that hath made us, and not we ourselves; we are his people, and the sheep of his pasture.
Ps. 100:1-3

Apple

Apple, apple, stay with me,
Apple, apple, you're green as a tree.
You're so good,
In a sweet way.
Should I eat you?
Yes I will!
Thank you God,
For making everything good.

By: Kadeedra Young

The Bible

God is good; the Bible is sweet,
God wants us to be good,
And Jesus does too.
I am glad God gave the Bible
To me and Jesus is glad for you too.

By: Kadeedra Young

Bless

Thank you God!
I'm blessed as I can be
That I belong to a family.
I love each and everyday.

God, Our Father,
Made them all.
I thank God;
He put the little stars in place.
I thank God; I'm glad
Dear God;
For I'm a child who still likes to run and play,
As I love to be thankful
Not ungrateful.

Thank you God!
I'm just as glad, as I can be.
To have a family
That you have given to me.

Thank you God!
For little girls and boys;
As I share my blocks and toys
With others, today.
As I can truly say, this is the best way
To say, I love you.

By: Wanda & Kadeedra Young

Thank You God

Thank You God
For eyes to see;
Thank you God
For ears to hear;
Thank you God
For a mouth to eat;
Thank you God
For feet to walk;
Thank you God
For hands to write;
Thank you God
For the lovely things
You made for me;
Thank you God!
Thank you God!
I'm just as glad as I can be
To have a family
That you have given to me.

By: Wanda Young

Blue

Roses are red,
Violets are blue,
I love Jesus,
And Jesus loves you.

By Kadeedra Young

All Things Bright And Beautiful

All things bright and beautiful
The Lord God made them all.
All creatures great and small,
And all things wise and wonderful,
The Lord God made them not to quarrel.

By: Wanda Young

Calls

Thank you God,
I'm big enough,
To put my toys away.
To help my dear mother
As I pray,
I better come quickly
When Dad calls.

By: Kadeedra Young

Thanksgiving Day

Just to give thanks, each and everyday.
By God's almighty hand,
We sow and weed the land.
Thus comes the golden harvest
A gift from Heaven above.
And so today we thank the Lord
For all His wondrous love.

By: Wanda Young

Jesus Loves Me

Jesus loves me,
The Bible tells me so.
Jesus loves me,
And all the little children do too.
Thank you, God,
For making us all, precious in His sight.

By: Kadeedra Young

Clay

The cat went up the tree,
The cat went down the tree.
I love to play,
Playing with clay
Can be fun,
But I need to pray.

By: Kadeedra Young

Help Me God To Close My Eyes When I Pray

Help me God, to close my eyes,
When I pray every day.
Help me God, to obey,
And pray what I'm supposed to do all day.

By: Kadeedra Young

Help Me To Obey

Help me to obey
Each and every day.
Help me to obey
JESUS,
God's only Son before I pray.

By: Kadeedra Young

Eat

Thank you God
For the world so great,
Thank you God
For the food we eat,
Thank you God
For the clothes we wear,
Thank you God
For the friends we meet,
Thank you God
For the birds that sing,
Thank you God
For our house we live in,
Thank you God, for every thing,
Thank you God
For your Son, Jesus,
I love each and every day.

By: Wanda Young

Thank You God

Thank You, God,
For the Bible is sweet to know.
Thank you God,
For the Bible I do know.
Thank you God,
That I tell my friends,
This is the only Book I read.

By: Kadeedra Young

Go To The Child

Go to the little child,
He will show you how to be saved today.
Go to this little boy,
He knows the truth, to those who will obey.

By: Kadeedra Young

Eyes

I thank God
I do the same thing every day.
I thank God
I do pray each and every way,
Not to disobey.

I thank God
For my mom and dad.
I thank God
For food to eat.
I thank You God
For giving me my mom and dad,
The health and strength so I can eat.

I thank God
For my friends, each boy and girl.
I thank You God
For my friends who like to share
The Bible with everyone.

By: Kadeedra Young

Thank You Jesus

I love my Jesus,
Thy throne on high, from far above,
With the bright morning star.
When I learn, all when I pray,
He looks on me with loving eyes,
Every day,
Thank You Lord.

By: Kadeedra and Wanda Young

Thank You God

Thank You God,
Unto You I pray, thou hast kept
Me all the day.

Thank You God,
Keep me ever in thy sight,
So to all I will say,
Stay close to God,
He will give
You light.

Thank You God
For children's prayer today,
For their loving hearts,
And their warm smiles,
I do pray.

Thank You God
For thy tender care,
To every girl and boy,
From God
The Father up above.

Thank You God, I pray.
Thank You God, I say.
Thank You God, I pray and I say,
I love You,
I love You God, all day.

Dear God,
All that I say,
Is a brand new day.
Dear God,
I love you,
In a very special way.

God is love,
God is up above,
God is for this little child,
With tender love,
Whose heart
Is filled with love.

By: Kadeedra and Wanda Young

Parents

I Thank God
For my mom;
She cooks today.
I Thank God
For my dad;
He went to work today.

By: Kadeedra Young

Oh, Lord

Have mercy upon me.
And be thou my helper.
And He will keep you
Forever,
Remember my child,
God will bless you.

By: Wanda Young

I'm Not Ashamed

My friend,
With my God
Beside me all the way.
I can sing
Praises to Him all the day.

By: Wanda Young

Gentle

Little children are joyful,
Little children, we adore thee,
Little children are God's gift;
Little children have their hearts
Opening to the Son above.

I give thanks to the Lord,
As my gentle Jesus hears me now.
As the morning sun appears,
This little child, give thanks so true.
As he sees another day, has come again
My Jesus,
I love you within my heart.

Thank you Lord for loving me,
Thank you Lord for answering this little child,
Thank you Lord for giving to us,
Thank you Lord for keeping me,
And thank you Lord,
For holding us all so gently in your arms.

Just a little child,
With a sweetest smile that care.
Just a little child, God will make it so.
Just a little child,
And all the things she says and does,
She wants Jesus to hear her prayer.

By: Wanda Young

Family

A family is a glorious thing,
Bringing joy to hearts;
A family is a gift,
To be surrounded with your love;
A family is to be treasured with comfort,
With a vision as we have been told,
As I give my all to Jesus above.

Oh, Lord, help me through the day
As I give my self to thee,
As I read His word
And take time to pray,
He gives me strength along the way
To lift me up with joy,
And fills my heart with a song.

My Saviour is always there
To help and to repair,
My Saviour is always there
To share our fears, to be aware;
My Saviour is always there
For gladness; my darling child,
Be good; let Him help you,
With thy tender care.

He always lightens up the load,
My child,
When we find that troubles seem too
Difficult to bear, and makes our lives
More wonderful.
My Saviour is always there.

By: Wanda Young

Sight

I pray dear Lord,
My soul He'll keep.
I pray dear Lord,
As He lay me down to sleep.
I pray dear Lord,
With His love be with me,
Through the night, with His gentle smile.
I pray dear Lord, as He blesses my child
With the morning light, Thank You my God,
For giving me sight.

Thank you God,
Help me to do the things I should,
To be to others so kind and good.
Thank you God
In all I do, and all I say,
I want to be more like you,
Each and every day

Thank you God
For the world so great,
Thank you God
For the food we eat.
Thank you God
For the clothes we wear.
Thank you God
For the friends we meet.
Thank you God
For everything.
Thank you God
For your Son Jesus,
Whom I love each and every day.

By: Wanda Young

Guide

Help me, dear Heavenly Father
And show me the way;
Help me, dear Heavenly Father
Guide and direct me,
All through this day;
Help me, dear Heavenly Father
As I go to prayer,
I'll learn how to pray.

By: Wanda Young

Rain

Thank you God
For the rain,
That falls for you and me.
Thank you God
As it helps all things to grow,
As I see along the way.

By: Kadeedra Young

For

Thank You God, for eyes to see.
Thank you God, for ears to hear.
Thank you God, for mouth to eat.
Thank you God, for feet to walk.
Thank you God, for hands to write.
Thank you God, for the lovely things
You made for me.
Thank you God!

By: Kadeedra and Wanda Young

The Best Way

Thank you God
For little girls and boys,
As I share my blocks and toys
With others today.
Thank you God
As I can pray, I know this is the
Best way to say today
I love you.

Thank you God
I'm big enough
To put my toys away.
Thank you God
To help my dear mother as I pray,
I better come quickly to Dad
when he calls.

We Thank You God
For your love, most of all.
We thank You God
For Your son JESUS,
Who died on the cross.

By: Kadeedra Young

Thanks

My child, we give thanks to the Lord
Each and every day,
For all his wondrous love;
Not just on Thanksgiving Day.
By God's almighty hand
A gift from heaven above.

By: Wanda Young

Thank God

I thank God
For my mommy and daddy,
So sweet and nice to me.
I thank God
For my mommy and daddy;
They are God's gift to me.

By: Kadeedra Young

I Need To Thank God

I need to thank God,
For giving me this day.
I need to thank God,
So I can pray.
I need to thank God,
Each and every day.

By: Kadeedra Young

I Thank God For My Birthday

I thank God
For my birthday
I do pray.
I thank God
For my birthday
Every year they are so dear,
For this time of year.

By: Kadeedra Young

I Pray

I pray the Lord
By keeping the doctor away;
Answer my prayer
I do pray.

By: Kadeedra Young

Bright Sunny Light

Thank You.
I Thank you Lord today.
As I pray,
To keep me through
The night,
And wake me up with
The bright, sunny light.

By: Wanda Young

Good

I thank God
For my brother,
I thank God
For my sister.
I do thank You Lord
Each and every day.

Good night God,
I love You;
Good night God,
I thank You;
Good night God,
I thank You, for letting me
See the morning light.

Good morning;
I love You.
Good morning;
I thank You.
Good morning,
Oh God,
I'm so thankful
To hear my child
Say good morning,
With a lovely smile.

The boy who had a smile,
Not a frown,
All the day long,
Not to play in the rain
Made him not to be ashamed,
But thanking God;
For all that He made.

The girl who had a gentle kind;
With so much on her mind,
She came back with a Bible
In her hand,
Thanking God for Ephesians 6:1.

I thank you God
For food to eat,
I thank you God
For bed to sleep,
I thank you God
For Mom and Dad,
Who are so sweet.

I love you God,
As I tell the story of Jesus;
I love you God
To tell this little child
From my heart every word was heard.
Do right my boy,
Do right my girl,
Do right if you could,
For Jesus sake, my darling girl
She is always making a cake
To do good.

Thank You God
Jesus grew as children do,
He played and ran
And worked hard too;
But one thing Kadeedra
Can say, He can bless you too.

Thank You God
Jesus grew as children do,
He played and cried
And worked hard too;
But one thing Nathaniel can say
He can bless Him too.

Thank You God
Help me to do the things I should
To be to others;
So kind and good.
Thank You God,
In all I do,
I want to be more like you,
Each and every day
I pray.

I pray dear Lord,
With his love be with me.
My soul He'll keep,
As he lay me down to sleep.
Through the night,
With his gentle smile,
With the morning light;
Thanking you Lord,
Forgiving me sight.

Help me, dear Father,
And show me the way;
Guide and direct me,
Through this day;
As I go to church
I'll learn how to pray.

Thank you God
For the rain,
My child for you and me.
Thank you God,
As it helps all things to grow
As I see each and everyday.

God made all the little children
He loves to show us what to do;
God loves the children
And I know He will save you to.

Thank you God
For children everywhere,
Thank you God
For your love up above;
As we sing with our voices
Given all praises to Him,
Thank you God very much indeed.

Thank goodness tonight
Where children are happy and bright;
As they say I need to do right
Anywhere and anytime;
My darling child,
Please go to bed and give thanks to
God each and every night.

Thank you God
Jesus loves all the little children;
Thank you God
For they are all precious, in his sight
And most of all God,
For your Son you gave to me.

Thank you God
For my sister,
Thank you God
For my brother,
Thank you God
For my sister and brother,
Whom I love to be
Around each and everyday.

Thank you God
For Grandma,
Thank you God
For Grandpa,
Thank you God
For grandma and grandpa,
Whom I loved to go and see
Not just on holidays.

Thank you God
For giving me a birthday,
I'm just like a child
With my toy.
Playing with my friends,
Singing happy birthday to you,
And God bless you too.

Dear Father
Bless the children
With thy word,
And guard us with our love
That we all can share.

Help me, Lord,
In my work and in my play,
Let me not forget to pray.
Help me Lord,
Now before I run to play.

Help me Lord,
Go with me through the day,
Be thou with me in the night.
Help me not to forget to pray,
As I see the morning light.

I Thank thee Lord for my rest.
This little child says;
I am blessed.
I thank thee Lord,
For my mother's prayer
With me, in thy care.

As I pray my heart is blessed
My dear child,
With thy presence, Oh Lord,
As we pray he sees,
And he is here and everywhere
I do adore.

By: Kadeedra and Wanda Young

My Dear Child

He prayeth all,
He loveth all,
He prayeth best,
He loveth best,
All things both great and small,
My dear child
He made and loveth all,
Most of all He prayeth all.

Praise God, from all blessing s flow,
Praise Him, all things below,
Praise God above, for Heavenly host,
Praise Father, Son, and the Holy Ghost.

Jesus, as I pray,
Jesus, as I say,
From thy home on high,
Look on me, with loving eyes,
Hear me when I pray.

Thank You God
God watches me all the day,
At home, at school and when we play.
Thank you God,
He watches with His eyes;
I do say
My child everyday.

Good morning,
As this child looks above,
And sees God's love;
Saying good morning,
Good morning, Jesus,
Waking up, on this bright sunny morning.

God of tenderness and praise
In all His wondrous ways,
To this little child.
When I'm weak I'm doing my best,
Mom, let me know I need to take a rest,
That giveth joy to all,
Although the place looks small,
Within the world to glow,
Wherever this loving child may go.

Jesus, listen to my prayer
Bless this little child.
Till the morning light
With a song in the night.
As she say; Oh Lord,
I cry to You listen please to my prayer.

God, bless this child
With gentle kindness,
Guide this child with tender love,
Show this child the way of brightness
From His smile up above.
Fill this little heart with love,
With the greatest part of God
My child,
Tis so sweet to trust in Jesus
The most of all,
As this child said, he heard my call.

Blessed is the Lord our King,
Lift up your head and sing,
He teaches us how to share,
He rules with kindness and with care.
Lift up your voice and sing my child,
Blessed is the Lord our King,
Look up in the sky above,
And see the glory of His love.

God, You made the sun and its
Golden light;
God, You made the moon and stars that
Come at night;
God, You made clouds that fill the sky;
God, You made birds with wings to fly.
God, You made me and my family.
God, we thank you in all we say and do.

By: Wanda Young

Thank You God Above

Thank you God above.
My house is blessed
by God above,
My room is filled with His wonderful love.
He protects me each and every way.
He keeps me night and day,
Thank you God above,
For your everlasting love.

By: Wanda Young

Seasons

God, I thank You for the seasons,
Summer, Fall, Winter and Spring.
God, I thank You for the joy that you bring,
God, I thank You for Summer heat both
Day and night;
Fall brings such a colorful sight,
Spring brings the fields with flowers
Wherever we go.
For Winter that blankets the land with snow,
No matter what the seasons bring,
All that you give to us;
As we lift our children's voices to God and sing.

By: Wanda Young

Manners

Good manners are a way
Of showing that you care.
As you grow don't say no,
You should also become more thoughtful,
By just saying my child
I'm thankful God.

By: Wanda Young

God's Care

Thank You God for taking care,
And making a world where we can share.
With hugs and kisses with those we love,
And with You, our God above.
Thank You God for caring,
Protecting, loving and leading, my child
Each and every day,
Thank you God, for everything.

By: Wanda Young

Creation

Thank You God for making the sun,
land and sea,
Thank You God for making the flowers,
Grass and trees,
Thank You God for making animals, both male
And female,
Both big and small;
And thank You God for making me, and my family
The most of all.

Green

Roses are red,
Grass is green.
I thank God each day,
That He made the Heaven and the Earth,
For boys and girls to see.

By: Kadeedra D. Young

Help

Help me, dear Father,
And show me the way;
Guide and direct me,
All through this day.

Thank you God
For the rain,
That falls for you and me.
Thank you God,
As it helps
All things to grow,
As I see each and everyday.

God made all the little children;
The Bible tells us what to do;
God loved the children.
I know He loves me to.

By: Kadeedra Young

Thank You God

For everything great and small.
Thank you God
For loving me the most of all.

By: Kadeedra Young

Help Me

Help me dear Heavenly Father
And show me the way;
Help me dear Heavenly Father
Guide and direct me,
All through this day.
As I go to church
I'll learn how to pray.

Thank you God
For the rain,
That falls for you and me.
Thank you God,
As it helps
All things to grow,
As I see along the way.

God made all the little children;
The Bible tells us what to do;
God loved the children
I know He loves me to.

We Thank you God
For everything, great and small.
We Thank you God
For Your Son Jesus the most of all.

By: Kadeedra and Wanda Young

Help Me To Obey

Help me to obey,
Each and every day.
Help me to obey
JESUS,
God's only son before I pray.

By: Kadeedra Young

I Thank God

I Thank God
For my mother,
Whom I have today
For not having my way.

By: Kadeedra Young

I Pray

I pray to the Lord,
and thank Him
for keeping me day by day.
He answers my prayers,
I love Him in every way.

By: Kadeedra and Wanda Young

Thank You God

Thank You God,
For loving me.
Thank You God
In a very special way,
When I pray,
All that I say.

By: Kadeedra Young

I Love You God

I love You God
For God so loved the world.
I do love to tell my
Friends,
In a very special way,
We do want to thank you God
Each and everyday.

By: Kadeedra Young

Kadeedra

My name is Kadeedra,
I love to pray,
I'm going to say,
Yes, to Jesus each and everyday.

By: Kadeedra Young

I Like To Play

I like to play,
I like to say,
I may go play, with my friends today.
I like to stay,
I like to pray,
I like to sing to my self every day.

By: Kadeedra Young

Jesus Loves Me

Jesus loves me so,
I do already know.
Jesus loves me,
And watches over us all the time.
Jesus loves all the children,
He wants us to be thankful,
And to obey my friend.

By: Kadeedra Young

Help Me To Obey

Help me to obey
Each and every day.
Help me to obey
My mommy and daddy,
I do love today.
Help me to obey God and Jesus,
In a very special way I pray.

By: Kadeedra Young

I Thank You Lord

I thank you Lord,
As I pray today,
That I'll like to say.

I thank you Lord,
Keep me through the night,
And wake me up with the morning light.

By: Kadeedra Young

I Need To Obey

I need to obey
God and Jesus in every way.
I need to obey
My mom and dad every day.

By: Kadeedra Young

I Need To Obey

I need to obey
In a way to pray.
I need to obey
So I can pray
All day.

By: Kadeedra Young

Let Others Share

Let others share your toys, my girl.
Do it, you will have fun,
For if you do it, your friend will be
Thanking God you did.

By: Kadeedra Young

Five Little Children

Said the first little child
With a loud voice, Oh, Dad I wish I could
Find Mom.
Said the second little child
With an quiet little voice, Oh, mom I wish I could
Find Grandma.
Said the third little child
With a shy little voice, Oh, Grandma I wish I could
Find Grandpa.
Said the Fourth little child
With a peaceful little voice, Oh, I wish I could
Find the fifth little child,
So I can tell him about JESUS.

By: Wanda Young

Thank You God

Thank You God
For children everywhere,
Thank You God
For Your love up above,
Thank You God
As we cry with our voices.
All agreed?
Thank You God very much indeed.

Thank You God
For this very night,
The stars in the sky
Are happy and bright.
Thank You God
For my darling child,
As I say do right,
In all of his might.
And give thanks to the Lord above
In sight.

Thank You God
For Jesus loves all the little children.
Thank You God
For they are all precious in his sight.
Thank You God
The most of all for the love
That you have given me.

Thank You God
For waking me up with the morning light.
Thank You God
For your goodness, each and every day.
Thank You God
I can go to church on Sunday morning,
With my friends, and we both can pray,
And hear the preaching today.

Thank you Jesus
For loving me.
Thank you Jesus
This I know.
Thank you Jesus
For the Bible tells me so.
Thank you Jesus
For heaven is up above.

Thank you God
For giving me a birthday.
Just like a child,
With his toy, playing with his friends
On his birthday, and Jesus saying
I can bless you too.

Help me Lord
In my work and play.
Help me Lord
Now before I run to play.
Help me Lord
Be thou with me the whole day.
Help me Lord
Let me not forget to pray.

Dear Father
Bless the children
With thy word.
And guard us with Your love,
That we all can share.

I thank thee Lord
For morning rest,
As this little child say;
Let me be blessed.
I Thank thee Lord
For my mother's prayer,
Is with me in God's care.

Give Him My Heart
Yes, what can I give Him
Children;
My Heavenly Father?
Give Him My Heart
As I hear the wonderful
Children,
Story about the wise man,
He said
I would do my part.

My dear child
As I pray my heart is blessed,
With thy presence Oh, Lord.
As I will say
My child,
God bless you and do His will.

Thank you God
A grey morning,
A little black bee,
A tiny purple violet,
A tiny green tree,
A red and white flag,
On a blue car port.
I thank you God
All these things, you gave to me
When you gave me eyes to see.

Jesus as I pray,
Jesus as I pray,
From thy home on high,
Look on me with thy loving eyes
Hear me when I pray.

Praise God, from all blessing flow
Praise Him all things below,
Praise God, above for Heavenly host Praise Father, Son,
And the Holy Ghost.

Thank You God
Unto You I pray,
Thou hast kept me all the day;
Keep me ever in thy sight so to all I
Will say please stay tight.

Thank You God,
God watches me all the day,
At home, at school and even when we play.
Thank you God,
He watches with a billion eyes,
I do say.

God is good,
God is grace,
God is so great in every way
And everyday I pray
Before I eat.

Jesus loves me
And I know its true,
Because He told me so
For his loving kindness and this
Is for you.

By: Kadeedra and Wanda Young

Pink

Roses are pink,
Plums are blue,
Jesus Christ loves you,
And sees everything I do too.

By: Kadeedra Young

Praise

Blessed is the Lord our King
Lift up your head and sing
My child,
He teaches us how to share,
He rules with kindness and with care.

By: Wanda Young

Hallelujah

Blessed is the Lord our King,
Lift up your voice and sing,
Hallelujah,
Hallelujah,
Look up in the sky above,
And see the Glory of his love,
My child.

By: Wanda Young

For The Bible

Thank You God
For the Bible,
It tells me how to be saved.
Thank You God
For God's book.
It tells me how to be good.
I will read God's book
In a very special way every day.

By: Kadeedra Young

Your Ways

Thank You God,
I have a father,
Who loves God's word.
Thank You God,
I have a mother,
Who learns about God's love.
Thank You God,
I have a brother and sister,
Who learn about Jesus.
Thank You God,
As we all read the Bible
And study,
And pray, and I love keeping Your ways.
Thank You God.

By: Wanda D. Young

Roses

Roses are red,
Violets are blue,
I want to go to Heaven
And see you too.

By: Kadeedra Young

We Shall See God

We shall see God
In our hearts.
We shall see God
On the cross.
We shall see God
Face to face,
Jesus Christ who loves me so.

By: Wanda Young

Serve The Lord

Serve the Lord
With all my heart.
Serve the Lord
With all my might.
Serve the Lord
With all my soul.
Serve the Lord
Boys and girls
With no end, my friend.
And jump up for joy!

By: Wanda Young

God Loves Me

God loves me,
For the Bible tells me so.
Red, and black, and white,
They are all precious in His might,
God loves them all in His sight.

By: Kadeedra Young

Speak

Obey your father and mother.
Always speak the truth.
Think before you speak.
Always keep your promises, my child.
Always do your best each and every day I pray.

By: Wanda Young

Sue

Roses are red,
Pumpkins are orange,
I can't change the color blue Sue,
Because that is only what God can do.

By: Kadeedra Young

The Sunshine

The sunshine
Through the earth.
The sunshine
Through me, every where you'll see
The sunshine is with me.

By: Kadeedra Young

Thank

I Thank God
I Thank God
For my Uncle,
We read a book together,
It was the Bible.

I Thank God
I Thank you God for
Grandma,
She is so sweet
She always make me go to sleep.

I Thank God
I Thank you God for
Mother,
Whom I have today,
For not having my way.

I Thank God
I Thank God
For my daddy,
He tells me Bible story,
That I love to tell
Every child today.

I Thank God
I thank God
For my brother,
He tells me to obey,
But he still disobey.

I Thank God
I thank God
For my sister,
She gave me warm milk
To drink,
And told me a Bible story, and put me to bed.

I Thank God
I thank God
For my Aunt,
She gives me hot chocolate,
And cookies,
And tells me to say nothing.

I Thank God
I do the same thing every day.
I thank God.
I do pray each and every way,
Not to disobey.

I Thank God
I thank God
For my mom and dad.
I thank God
For food to eat.
I thank You God
For giving me my mom and dad,
The health and strength so I can eat.

I Thank God
I thank God
For my friends, each boy and girl.
I thank You God
For my friends who like to share
The Bible with everyone.

By: Kadeedra and Wanda Young

Thank You God

Thank You God,
For the Bible is sweet to know.
Thank You God,
For the Bible I do show.
Thank You God,
That I tell my friends,
This is the only book I read.

By: Kadeedra and Wanda Young

Go To The Child

Go to the little child,
He will show you how to be saved today.
Go to this little boy,
He knows the truth, to those who will obey.

By: Kadeedra and Wanda Young

Thank You Jesus

I love my Jesus,
Thy throne on high, from far above,
With the bright morning star.
When I learn, all when I pray,
He looks on me with loving eyes, every day,
Thank You Lord.

By: Kadeedra and Wanda Young

Thanks

Thank You God,
Unto You I pray, thou hast kept
Me all the day.
Thank You God,
Keep me ever in thy sight,
So to all I will say,
Stay close to God,
He will give you light.

Thank You God
For children's prayer today,
For their loving heart,
And their warm smiles,
I do pray.
Thank You God
For thy tender care,
To every girl and boy,
From God
The Father up above.

Thank You God I pray,
Thank You God I say,
Thank You God I pray and say,
I love You,
I love You God all day and all the way.

I thank You Lord today,
As I pray,
To keep me through
The night,
And wake me up
With the bright sunny light.

By: Wanda Young

Daddy

I have a Daddy
Most of all,
He reads from the Bible,
God's word,
And I learn about his loving ways.

By: Kadeedra Young

Tree

Tree, tree go away,
Come to my house,
Some other day.
I'm sorry; that I grew here,
That's okay you are a
Fun little tree.
Thank you God
For this little tree,
That you made for me.

By: Kadeedra Young

Yellow

Roses are yellow,
Oranges are orange,
And very sweet.
I can tell you today,
Who is sweeter than oranges;
My friend,
Jesus Christ.

By: Kadeedra Young

Help Me God To Be More Like You

Help me God to be more like You,
I do pray.
Help me God to be more like You,
And obey, I do say.
Help me God to be more like You,
In a very special way.

By: Wanda Young

Courtesy

Courtesy to my loving child,
Being thoughtful,
Being cheerful,
Being respectful,
Being polite,
Being kind,
Being patient,
Being thankful
For everything for this dear child
who wants to know COURTESY.

By: Wanda Young

Biography

Wanda Young and Kadeedra Young
give thanks to their
Lord and Saviour Jesus Christ
for His grace, love, and mercy.
They rejoice in the opportunity to serve
and share the love of Christ
through this collection,
"Joyful Poems For Children."

Mrs. Young and Kadeedra ask for your prayers
and offer their appreciation,
for your support and encouragement.
God in His great mercy gave
the gift of poetry to Mrs. Young and Kadeedra.
They share the gift with you.
Thanks be to God for all of His unspeakable gifts.

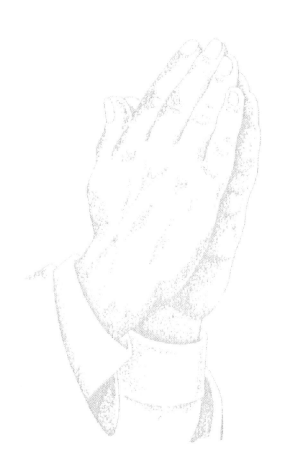